# mindfulness
## and Sport Psychology for Athletes:
*Consider Awareness Your Most Important Mental Tool*

by Kristine M. Eiring, PhD and Colleen M. Hathaway, DC

Copyright © 2012 Kristine M. Eiring, Ph.D.,
and Colleen M. Hathaway, D.C., Madison, WI
www.dreiring.us and www.innergyllc.com
www.mindfulnessforathletes.us
Facebook: mindfulness for athletes

Second Edition.
All rights reserved worldwide.
No part of this e-book may be used or reproduced in any manner whatsoever without the written permission of the Authors.
For information address the Authors in care of:
Innergy, LLC
715 Hill St., Suite 260
Madison, WI 53705

# Chapter 1
## Mindfulness and Sport Psychology for Athletes

This book is for athletes who want to build a mental practice as part of their overall training program. Many athletes understand that the mental aspects of training and competing are just as important as the physical aspects. The concepts in this book are designed for all athletes and can be used for building your own individualized mental training program as it relates to your sport.

Here is what you will learn:
- What mindfulness is and how it will benefit you
- How to use mindfulness with sport psychology tools
- Mindful recovery following practices and performance

---

*"What percent of your game is mental? Maybe as much as 90 percent. You make the mental choice every day to train your body. Make the same choice to train your brain."*
-Kris Eiring, PhD

---

The information in this book is on the cutting edge of sport psychology, because mindfulness is the key factor for a successful mental program. Many sport psychology books and workbooks provide a basic outline of various mental skills that athletes can use to help their performance; however, this book is different because it links mental skills with the concept of mindfulness. The basic idea of mindfulness is simple:

## You can change habits only through awareness.

By following the suggestions in this book, an athlete can learn the skill of awareness and use it to make quick mental decisions that drastically change thought processes. The end result of a new thought process is enhanced athletic performance. Mindfulness is a powerful vehicle for change because it brings the athlete to the only moment of importance—the present moment.

## A Brief History

In the 1950s, psychology was focused on observable behavior. Psychologists primarily looked at what happened before a behavior (antecedents) and after a behavior (consequences) to understand actions and reactions. For example, if athletes had anger management problems, it was because something in the environment had provoked their behavior or because it was being rewarded. The treatment for the anger problem was to change the environmental factors triggering it.

Around the 1970s, a growing number of psychologists began to put forth the idea that we need to look inside the individual, not just outside, as a means to understanding behavior. What is the athlete thinking? What are his or her beliefs? What is this person saying to himself? This became known as cognitive psychology. Cognitive anger-management therapy might have looked at helping the athlete change his or her thoughts about the situation. The environment was not the only factor to consider; the athlete's beliefs were important, too.

Later the two approaches to understanding behavior were joined, and cognitive-behavioral theories and therapies developed. Psychologists began looking at both the environment and the athlete's thought process to fully understand behavior. Many sport psychology techniques have a foundation in this approach, such as imagery, goal setting, and self-talk skills.

Today, there is a growing movement toward mindfulness as a practice and tool in psychology (Cormier and Nurius, 2008). A mindfulness-based approach might be considered the next generation in psychology. The objective of this approach is to help people become more aware of their thoughts instead of trying to eliminate certain thoughts. The goal of this book, then, is to help athletes learn and understand mindfulness, because it is the foundation of many other sport psychology tools.

## What Is Mindfulness?

Mindfulness is both a way of being or living and a tool one can use to build mental flexibility. What does this mean to athletes?

According to Jon Kabat-Zinn, author of numerous mindfulness books, mindfulness is about paying attention in a particular way, on purpose, in the present moment. There is also a nonjudgmental quality to it. Mindfulness is being in the present moment, which means not dwelling on past events (such as mistakes) or anticipating future events, such as winning or losing. In fact, when athletes describe being "in the zone," they often describe a sense of being fully aware and present.

The quickest tool to access the present moment is the breath.

---

*Feelings come and go like clouds in a windy sky. Conscious breathing is my anchor.*
~Thich Nhat Hanh

---

▲ For example, imagine that a triathlete starts a competition with the swim, but she doesn't like her performance or time. She begins her cycling but continues to think about her poor swim time and how she should have done better. Soon she loses focus on her cycling form and begins to perform poorly. When she's done biking, she moves on to the run. Now she is mad that she didn't mentally let go of her swim performance sooner and messed up her cycle time. So she stays in the past for her run, too.

This athlete lost the present moment, and it affected her performance. How could she have used mindfulness as a tool?

The first step is tuning into the breath, which brings the athlete immediately to the present moment, setting the stage for her next step or decision. Breathing helps the mind be calm yet alert. By focusing first on breathing, an athlete can then look at a range of possibilities and choose the best mental approach for her situation.

Many athletes "hope" to experience ease and flow while training or competing. When you "hope," you leave doubt in your mind. Instead, empower yourself and learn methods to help move you in the direction of flow or the "zone," where you are fully present in the moment. Mindfulness is a tool that can help take you to that place.

**Foundation of Mindfulness**
In his book *Full Catastrophe Living*, Jon Kabat-Zinn outlines the foundation principles of mindfulness. Several of these principles are important for athletes of all levels to understand and build into their mental game.

The first principle is **non-judging**. We have constant streams of thoughts about experiences occurring in our lives. Many of us lose time and energy judging those experiences as good or bad. Kabat-Zinn points out how this creates a "yo-yo mind," or what might also be labeled "mental teeter-tottering." When judging an experience, a person may have an "in your head argument," going back and forth about that experience—or for an athlete, a workout or performance.

Many athletes also "yo-yo" when thinking about thinking. Many have been told by coaches to be positive or to not think too much. The problem with this advice is that many athletes don't know where to put their attention. That internal struggle results in wasted mental energy and a lack of awareness of the present moment, which contributes to a less than ideal performance.

The second important principle is **acceptance**. Kabat-Zinn describes this as seeing things as they are or exist now, and knowing not to waste time thinking about events that have already occurred. A basketball player who misses an easy lay-up in a game may dwell on the missed shot. A runner or swimmer who doesn't like a lane assignment may stew over how the lane isn't the right one. In these instances, accepting the present moment or situation is a valuable skill that can help an athlete direct his or her focus. This quick and simple skill lays the foundation for redirecting thought processes and making the next best choice in the moment.

Finally, the third important principle is **patience**. Non-judgment and acceptance are valuable tools in building a strong mental game in sport, but developing those tools takes time, practice, and patience.

## Mindfulness and Meditation

By engaging in a meditation practice, an athlete can learn and apply principles toward building a mindful approach to sport. Mindfulness is a skill, and meditation is a practice you can use to build this skill. Both are important for athletes. There are many different types of meditation practices, and you may want to take a class or read books to find a practice that works well for you.

At the present time there is substantial research being done in the field of meditation. It is being studied in relation to positive mental health, anxiety management, stress management, and pain management. For more information, consider exploring the work of Richard Davidson, Ph.D., at the University of Wisconsin-Madison. He is one of the leading researchers in the world in this field and has founded the Center for Investigating Healthy Minds. You might also read *Full Catastrophe Living* by Jon Kabat-Zinn.

### Personal Reflections

While I was competing as a sprinter at the University of Wisconsin-Madison, I developed my own mental tools to help me with my starts for the indoor 55-meter dash. I used a two-step process to help me focus. First, while standing at the starting line, I would say over and over "line first," which meant to me to cross the finish line first. Once we were in the starting blocks, I would switch to "gun," as all I wanted at that point was to hear the gun shot and to blast out of the blocks first. I didn't know it at the time, but I was using a basic mindfulness technique, a mantra, so my thoughts could be no other place—not on other sprinters, not on my time, not on my judgment of my readiness. I wanted a single focus. This helped me stay in the present moment and not have anxiety about the finish. I was using a mantra, a form of meditation, and it helped me not to over-think or focus on anxious thoughts.

*– Kristine M. Eiring, Ph.D.*

● Playing point guard on a college basketball team meant I needed to think through many situations at any given moment. One of my positive thinking tools developed accidentally my sophomore year while listening to the national anthem. I had three thoughts rolling through my head, and I found myself counting the stars on the American flag while I was listening to the anthem. I repeated, "hustle, defense, shoot" star after star. By the end of the song I had run through all fifty stars, and a new mindful, positive thinking routine was born. I continued this through my entire college basketball career and still find myself doing this while watching games today.

*– Colleen M. Hathaway, D.C.*

**Foundational Tool of Mindfulness**

Mindfulness is knowing what mental tools and skills to use to help bring you, the athlete, back to the present moment—the moment that is most important for performance. Mindfulness is the key to making the most of the basic sport psychology tools of positive thinking, self-talk, goal setting, imagery, and recovery.

# Chapter 2
## Mindfulness and Thinking

*"You are only as strong as you are flexible in mind and body."*
-Colleen Hathaway, D.C.

Many athletes confuse mindfulness with meditation and think the goal is to not have any thoughts. But you will always have thoughts. The goal is not to stop thinking but to have awareness of, and flexibility in, your thinking. Through mindfulness, you will realize that you have choices and can decide which thoughts to focus on and follow.

Did you know that you dialogue with yourself on just about every topic throughout almost every day? You have good thoughts, neutral thoughts, and critical thoughts. Thinking is a habit—something you do automatically.

Statistics vary, but the National Science Foundation put out a report that indicated we think between 12,000 to 50,000 thoughts per day (http://www.sentientdevelopments.com/2007/03/managing-your-50000-daily-thoughts.html). We tend to dwell in the past or on the future, obsessing about mistakes we made, battling guilt, planning ahead, or worrying.

As athletes, we think constantly during training and while competing. Those thoughts can be helpful or not helpful, and we may not even know how our thoughts are influencing us from moment to moment. Many athletes hear from their coaches, "You need to think positive!" However, many athletes do not know how to move into positive thought.

Mindfulness is a skill that helps athletes gain awareness about their internal chatter. We often have numerous thoughts occurring very quickly. Some we follow and some we do not. Mindfulness is about utilizing and giving more attention to those thoughts that are typically associated with better performance.

**Thoughts: Think of Them Like a Traffic Light**
Our minds can operate like traffic lights, switching from green to red and red to green. Green thinking means that you are in the flow, that you are present in your workout or competition. Red thinking is dwelling on what's wrong, worrying about events in the future, or focusing on all the things you don't like.

Research is showing a mind-body connection and it seems that the more stressful the thoughts we have, the more stress hormones we produce (Sternberg, 2000). This means that if you think negatively, your body experiences more tension, which may lead to a poor workout or competition. When you start thinking negatively, you likely begin to picture a less than ideal performance. Then you struggle inside, trying to eliminate the image mentally. This creates resistance or tension in your mind and body. By thinking "red" thoughts, you are basically holding yourself back and not using your mental tools in a helpful way. When you tell someone to think of a pink elephant or to not think of a pink elephant, the result is the same. Both think of the pink elephant! You must direct your mind.

Awareness is the tool that can help you switch those red thoughts into something more directive or helpful. This is a big step in reaching your goals more easily. The key is mindfulness, or the awareness that you need to switch those thoughts.

Personal Reflections

● I have a clear memory of "red thinking" while I was competing in the indoor USA track meet in Madison Square Garden, New York. I had qualified to compete in the indoor 60-meter dash. The first thing I checked when I arrived was the heat that I was running in. When I saw all the big-time sprinters in my heat (such as Evelyn Ashford and Chandra Cheeseborough), I instantly said to myself, "I don't belong here." Guess what? I didn't make the semi-finals. I never switched my thinking. It stayed red, and I didn't know what to do to help myself. I lost my confidence.

*– Kristine M. Eiring, Ph.D.*

● I, too, have a clear memory of "red thinking" while playing in the NCAA basketball tournament in Iowa. There was a minute and a half left in a game that was tied. I remember being fouled and going to the free throw line, and my thoughts were, "I'm not the right person to be at the line. I hope I don't miss." I **did** miss. I didn't have the awareness to switch my thoughts quickly, and I stayed with red thoughts. My brain looked for ways to help me miss, because that was what I was telling it to do.

*– Colleen M. Hathaway, D.C.*

**Pushing Negative Thoughts Away Is NOT the Answer**
When negative thoughts pop up, many athletes immediately try to push the thoughts away or cover them up with "green" or positive thinking. This may help, but sometimes the scales tip and the athlete may try too hard to be positive, resulting in an internal conflict. You may have an unwinnable in-your-head argument between your "good guy" and your "bad guy." You might say to yourself, "I shouldn't think this, but I am thinking this!"

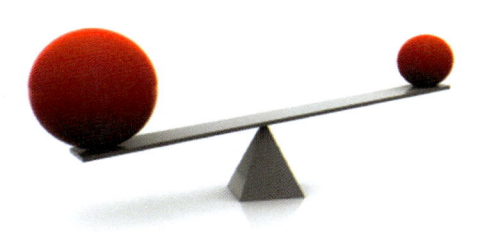

Why is this an unwinnable argument? Because you cannot lie to yourself. You cannot be disingenuously positive at a time when you don't like your performance or you know you aren't performing at your best. It's hard to believe positive thinking in that moment.

So what do you do?

> *"If there weren't yellow lights, there would be a lot of crashes."*
> –Kelly Hathaway, age 9

**Think Yellow Thoughts**
Recall for a moment the ideas presented earlier on yo-yo mind or teeter-totter thinking. This is when an athlete swings from positive to negative thoughts, or visa versa. It might be helpful to think of non-judgment thinking as "yellow," like those yellow traffic lights. Yellow thoughts are neutral, such as counting steps or simply focusing on one task or action (e.g., breathing or pumping arms).

In their book *The Psychology of Enhancing Human Performance*, authors Gardner and Moore focus on this very idea. They write that we must naturally check in with our inner self and engage in a self-adjustment at times. However, athletes become more dysfunctional in terms of performance when they focus on thoughts of perceived deficits or self-doubt. The functional performer is the one who can tune in to adjustments and remain neutral (yellow thinking) before ultimately shifting back into mindfulness (green thinking).

How can you apply yellow thinking and mindfulness to your sport?

## The Three A's: The Mindfulness Solution

Here are the steps:

1. AWARENESS. Be aware of what is happening (mindfulness).
2. ACCEPTANCE. Accept what is happening. Don't argue about it in your head.
3. ACTION. Leave positive and negative thinking—or judgment—out of it. Get off the teeter-totter. How? Engage in yellow thinking by giving your mind an action step. Become task focused.

The first step is being **aware** of what you are saying to yourself or the nature of your thinking. *This is mindfulness.* You can do this by just taking a deep breath and observing. Imagine you are in a cloud, looking down on yourself and listening to your thoughts. What do you hear? If you are hearing more red thoughts, such as "I can't do this" or "Everything is horrible," then move on to step two.

The second step is **accepting** that you are thinking red thoughts. Fighting with these thoughts is unproductive. Acceptance means naming the thoughts. Most people think things such as "I can't do this." Change that thought to "I am thinking I can't do this."

## "I am *thinking* I can't do this" is different from "I can't do this."

This is a small but very important difference. You cannot change all of your thinking patterns, but you can recognize a thought, and you can choose to follow it or not.

The way to shift these conditioned "I can't . . ." thoughts is through a mindful and non-judgmental awareness, by training your mind through repetition of the mantra "I am only thinking that I can't." Quickly, a realization will occur:

You do not need to believe everything that you are thinking!

*"We never talk about what we can't do. We talk about 'here's what we need to do, so let's go out and do it.' "*
– Brad Stevens, Butler basketball coach,
quote from Wisconsin State Journal 3/24/11

Finally, the third step to mindfulness is **action**. Recognize that you have a choice in changing your focus or thoughts. Action gives you other options.

One of the best actions you can take to change your cycle of thinking is strong physical exertion, such as a quick burst of sprinting or one minute of pedaling hard on a stationary bike. This produces testosterone, which stimulates the frontal lobe of the brain and paves the way for more clear thinking.

Other actions may include taking a deep breath to relax or asking yourself a good question. Ask, "Is there something I can think of that's more helpful?" or "What can I think of that would be neutral (yellow)?" Your brain will want to help you answer that. It works like a search engine on your computer.

The simplest path to a yellow thought is accomplished by asking this question:

## What's Important Now (W.I.N.)?

W.I.N. is a simple yet powerful acronym that comes from Lou Holtz, the famous Notre Dame coach. By asking this question, you can begin guiding yourself back to the present moment, or at least to a neutral place. Answer the question by saying things such as, "I can refocus. I am okay. I can do this. I can take it one step at a time."

Through mindfulness, you can accept that you are thinking in a certain way and also that you have the choice to follow a different thought. This realization and acceptance all happens at the speed of light!

Remember the triathlete who was angry about her swim performance? She could have used mindfulness and "switch thoughts" to help her focus. When she started her cycle part of the race, she could have told herself, "The swim is done. My focus is the cycle right now." If she had negative thoughts, she could acknowledge those thoughts: "I am thinking this was not a good swim, but I can evaluate that later, when the competition if finished. Right now, the cycle needs my attention. I can focus on my breath or my legs and get into my rhythm." Through awareness, she could accept that she is being negative and then switch her thoughts, thus preventing a possible internal argument in her head and bringing her back to the task at hand—the present moment!

Personal Reflections

🟢 After my sprinting career in college, I started to do some road races and also began to swim more. Both of these activities were a big mental switch for me because there was more time to think in training and competing. Sometimes when I was distracted and telling myself "I don't want to do this" or "I'm not good at this," I would switch my thinking to neutral and begin to count steps between markers, look at shoe colors of other runners, or even add up house address numbers in my head. All of these neutral thoughts were and still are really helpful in getting me to a more mindful mental place, which helps me run or swim better.

*– Kristine M. Eiring, Ph.D.*

🟢 In my early thirties, I began participating in longer endurance events. I had a difficult time "minding my mind." I would say things like, "I don't like running. My knees hurt. This is boring. I want to be somewhere else. I miss my teammates!" I experienced a dramatic shift in my thinking shortly following a seminar in mindfulness. It was there that I learned about "watching" my mind and not believing everything my mind was saying. I began to pay attention to my thoughts and name them as just thoughts. I learned how to tune into my breathing and stay with the exercise I was choosing. I have since completed numerous endurance events that I would not have been able to do without mindfulness.

*– Colleen M. Hathaway, D.C.*

## Thinking as It Relates to Our Inner and Outer Environments

When we discuss negative and positive thinking, be aware that this applies both to analyzing ourselves and our outer environments, such as playing conditions. For example, you might have feelings of nervousness while competing. You might notice this and begin to think about it and judge it: "Oh, no! If I'm nervous, I might play bad." You have attitudes and thoughts about your "inner world" and physical sensations, and then you dialogue with yourself about this. At the same time, you might also have attitudes and self-talk about others around you. You focus on your opponent and talk to yourself about how good he or she is looking during warm-ups. You start to think about yourself and question if you look that ready. Both instances involve you going into your "head" and having a dialogue. Both instances involve judgment, and both can be addressed via the three A's: awareness, acceptance, and action.

## Building Reminders into Your Mental Practice

We've been recycling since at least the 1970s, but only recently has it become a world priority. One of the reasons for the change is that we see so many reminders about it. Think about the garbage bins used for recycling, the television ads, the signs at work and school, and the movement to conserve. We have constant reminders to change our behavior, so we are getting much better at "thinking green." We are becoming more mindful of our choices regarding how we treat our earth and environment.

This same idea relates to sport psychology. If you are to become mentally strong, you need not only tools and techniques, you need *reminders* to help apply focused "green" thinking. Focus is a mental muscle, which means you strengthen it by learning to redirect your attention over and over again. Visual reminders, such as notecards, colored shoestrings or a dot on a hockey stick, build mental strength by giving you a focus and telling your brain instantly to focus.

Research indicates that to learn and apply one must repeat and practice. If this sounds like your basic training, it is. The mind and body are connected through repetition. The more we see, the more we do, and the more efficient we become.

Building reminders into your mental practice is like making a grocery list. You know what you need but sometimes forget. The same thing happens with mental skills. You understand the concepts, but you need to see them over and over to build a strong mental set. It is like doing weight repetitions to build muscles.

Facts:
- If you want to learn something, you must repeat it for better memory.
- If you want to learn something, you should use visual reminders to help you get better with the mental game.
    - Have note cards or sticky notes with your reminders for mental focus on them, and place them where they will be seen every day.
    - Hang posters or notes in your locker room, locker, or car, or on your bathroom mirror.
    - Wear a colored shoestring or wristband that acts as a reminder of your focus. Every time you see this, your brain will make a connection to your desired outcome.

---

*"To build mental strength, you need to have repetition."*
–Kristine M. Eiring, Ph.D.

---

Use this chart to list the helpful thoughts and actions that you want to remember:

| Helpful positive thought: | Helpful action: |
|---|---|
| I can do this | Breathe. |
| I'm okay. | Count. |
| Focus. | Focus on a spot or shoe or shirt. |
| I believe in me | Look at something in your environment. |
| Other helpful positive thoughts: | Other helpful actions: |
| _____ | _____ |
| _____ | _____ |
| _____ | _____ |
| _____ | _____ |

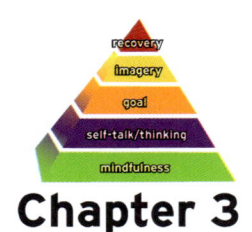

# Chapter 3
## Mindfulness and Goal Setting

*"A goal is a desired result that a person envisions or plans and commits to achieve—a personal desired end-point in some sort of assumed development."*
—Wikipedia

How can it be that athletes who achieve the same result can have two completely different reactions? One might be elated while the other might feel defeated. It seems that how one defines "success" might be closely aligned to the type of goals one sets or is driven to achieve.

Many athletes are driven to improve certain skills and/or to beat their opponent to gain accolades. These two drives to pursue excellence often co-exist, and it may be important to develop both (Eliot, 2005). "The behavior of coaches, parents, peers, and teammates has a powerful effect on the athlete's understanding of what achievement means. These individuals create an environment around the athlete that's known as the motivational climate" (Harwood, 2005, p. 23). Depending on whether these people reinforce high effort, constant cooperation, and shared contributions; give punishment or negative feedback for mistakes; or give special treatment to star players, a different climate is created. That climate may impact what kind of goals an athlete develops and values.

It seems that our goals can be task driven or ego driven, according to achievement-goal theory (Harwood, 2005). Athletes who have task-oriented perspectives are more concerned with effort and believe abilities can be improved. Athletes with ego-oriented perspectives see ability as somewhat "set," and they tend to compare themselves more to others. They want to show what they can do, sometimes even at the expense of effort (Harwood, 2005). There may be some benefit in the pursuit of beating an opponent, of working toward "winning" as a main goal. However, for athletes wanting long-term success, the development of task- or achievement-oriented goals is important (Eliot, 2005).

To date, research seems to support many advantages of having task-oriented goals. An athlete who has this perspective may engage less often in judgment or negative thinking and may therefore be more mindful. The thrill of getting better on certain aspects of one's game or sport is important in motivation, and improving skills can ultimately lead to passing your competitor in a race, too.

Goals help direct our attention and focus. Having goals also plays an important part in successful performance because we usually "rehearse" goals in our working memory. Athletes rehearse goals both by talking to themselves about their goals (self-talk) and by picturing their goals (imagery) (Cormier and Nurious, 2008).

Goals also help athletes determine the actions they will take to reach their desired outcome. In this way, goals help create the expectation of success as athletes design action plans (workouts) in order to meet the desired goals.

**Types of Goals: Outcome and Process**

Athletes and coaches set training and competition goals. Training goals often involve working on and achieving certain set points, such as lifting a certain amount of weight, reaching a particular shot or batting percentage, or hitting a certain number of fairways in a golf round. These types of goals are called **outcome goals**. Most athletes are aware of these types of goals and often have long-term and short-term outcome goals set for a season.

What are your outcome goals? Consider certain season goals or competition goals:

1. _____
2. _____
3. _____

There are times when **process goals** may be just as important, or even more important. Process goals mean exactly what the name implies—picking one specific action to turn your attention to and using that action as a guideline for improvement. Process goals are about how you're doing something, not about the final outcome. They're especially helpful if you aren't performing at the level you want or if you continually feel disappointed with your outcome.

Mindfulness creates awareness as to what types of goals you need to focus on—outcome or process. But setting process goals ultimately helps you achieve outcome goals and can help with confidence building, as well. It's sometimes more helpful to think of how you will move through your performance and to let the end result take care of itself. Here are a few examples of process goals:

- A runner chooses to focus on arm movement for a sustained time during a workout.
- A basketball player practicing free-throw shooting concentrates on wrist follow-through.
- A rower focuses on an efficient pulling technique for an entire practice.

What process goals can you set for yourself? You may have different process goals for each practice or even for a competition.

1. _____
2. _____
3. _____

Mindfulness can be part of this goal-setting process. You need to remember and stay aware of your goals. Brain research shows that if we see something frequently, like a daily reminder of a goal, we are more likely to remember it.

That means you need to have visual reminders of your goals, preferably reminders that you will see throughout the day. When you see a visual reminder, you can say to yourself, "I'm working on that." It's like a training workout that is posted on a wall. If you forget your workout routine, you see the posted moves and your brain reacts with, "Oh, yeah, now I remember."

Goal reminders can be very simple visual cues, such as a swatch of color or an image on a hockey stick or a softball bat. Some people even wear different colored shoestrings so that they can look down, see the colors, and be reminded of their goal. Goal reminders can also serve as reminders to be in the present moment, which is a good practice.

Choose a goal reminder that is visual, and see how it helps you. What will it be?

## Personal Reflection

● Part of the reason a coach outlines a workout is to give structure and goals for the practice. A specific outcome goal for sprinting was sometimes completing several practice 100-meter sprints, each in a certain time. Process goals included high knees and strong arms without a specified time.
– Kristine M. Eiring, Ph.D.

● Goals are vital for success in any athletic event. I have come to appreciate the idea that outcome goals give me a specific thing to focus toward—a number goal. In contrast, process goals remind me to pay close attention to the needs of my body during a training or competition and to adjust accordingly.
– Colleen M. Hathaway, D.C.

Whether you set outcome or process goals, make sure that they are:

## ARMS

- ❏ **A**ction oriented: Know exactly what you are going to do.
- ❏ **R**ealistic: Set goals that you can attain but that make you reach slightly for your next level.
- ❏ **M**easurable: If your goal is truly measurable, someone else should be able to tell when you've met your goal.
- ❏ **S**equential: Just as you break down a play or a routine into parts, consider having smaller goals that build on one another and allow you to work toward a bigger goal.

# Chapter 4
## Mindfulness and Imagery

Imagery is an important tool in sports. Some refer to it as visualization or as "mental rehearsal." Imagery is different from self-talk because with imagery, an athlete is using mental pictures and not words to create an image in the mind; but imagery and self-talk often go hand in hand.

Why is imagery important? Consider this: Important scientific data has been released from the National Institutes of Health confirming that the mind and body function as one. Researchers have found, via extensive animal and human studies, that stem cells migrate from the bone marrow into the brain and become new neurons (Holzel, et al., 2011). In essence, the growth of brain cells never stops. This means you can learn, change, and grow with each new thought or image you have during the day. These new cells give rise to new thoughts, and mindful images are critical to what you create. You are what you think!

A French pharmacist in the 1800s is credited for helping promote the idea of imagery. He touted it as a method to aid relaxation and thought it was important to think positive and not dwell on illnesses. He believed the power of the imagination can exceed the will and that it is easier to imagine relaxation spreading throughout your body than to "will it" (Davis, Eshelman, & McKay, 2006).

For athletes, it is important to use imagery as part of their mental game. Mental imagery can be used to recall and review a best performance, see yourself being successful, or practice a new skill in your mind. Just as athletes might learn by watching a film of other great athletes in their sport, an athlete can also use his or her own mind to visualize a performance.

Some researchers have found that your brain lights up in the same way whether you are experiencing an event or simply visualizing it. This means that it is very important to visualize what you want to have happen. For example, some divers mentally rehearse their dive twists and moves prior to actually doing them. Runners see themselves in a race, practicing tactical moves in their minds. Studies seem to show that successful athletes use imagery more extensively than less successful athletes (Vealey & Greenleaf 2006). An interesting study done by Gregg and Hall (2006) showed that for some golfers that as their handicap increased their use of visualization decreased.

Imagery can be used to:

- Recall past successes and help build confidence
- Rehearse a move, play, or overall game plan
- Remain focused and stay present by seeing plays develop and unfold
- Remind yourself of your goal by seeing it happen in your mind

Using this skill in the best way often requires mindfulness. One image can create an entire story and an incredible amount of self-talk. Do you want to rehearse what you did wrong? No! You may want to review what you did as a way to make corrections, but you do not want to go over and over what went wrong. Unfortunately, many athletes do this and don't know how to break the habit. They finish a competition and focus on their mistakes.

Replaying mistakes is like self-punishment. Some athletes believe that if they make themselves feel bad enough, they can somehow make up for the mistake. Do you do this?

**Moving beyond a mistake and recovering mentally is more important than replaying the mistake in your mind.** Why? Because if you continue to dwell on mistakes or on outcomes that you don't want, your brain might help you follow those negative pathways. Instead, when you make a mistake, learn from it. Decide what you do want and visualize that action or outcome. Your brain will then know what it is that you want to accomplish. Mindful imagery is a learned skill that helps good athletes become great!

Knowing your brain is growing every day is another reason to make a change in your thinking. Feed your mind healthy thoughts to help build new pathways. Apply the three A's of mindfulness:

- Awareness of a poor performance
- Acceptance of the fact that this was not the best you could do
- Action, or visualization of what you want to have happen so that you are in a better place to make it happen in the future

▲ Again, remember the triathlete? When she finished her race, she could have asked herself three questions: What went well mentally and physically? What did not? What corrections would I like to make? She could then visualize the corrections. This would be a much better way to learn and recover, and get ready for the next competition. She could pave the way for how she wants to perform.

We all develop patterns, ways of doing things, which may be helpful or not. To change habits, your mind has to help your brain. You can train new brain pathways, but you have to feed your brain consistent positive images, self-talk, and behaviors. Retraining your brain is like learning to bat with your left hand when your right hand is dominant. You can do it with practice, imagery, and self-talk. It may be uncomfortable, but it is possible. This is your mind and brain working together.

Ask yourself these questions before you practice imagery:
- What image do I want of myself when I train?
- What new skill do I want to visualize doing well?
- Prior to competing, what do I want to visualize?
    - Picture yourself performing successfully. Visualize or see yourself meeting process goals.
    - Try to place yourself in the visualization rather than just seeing yourself doing something. Incorporate all of your senses: sight, smell, touch, sound, and taste.
    - Mindfully state what you want: "I want to..."

Most commonly, imagery is used in sport is to recall a "best performance." Follow the instructions below for this exercise. It works well if you write your answers first and then visualize the experience.

1. Recall your best performance, a time when you were performing with ease.
2. Involve all of your senses: sights, sounds, and smells.
3. Ask yourself these questions: Where was I? Who else was there? What were the conditions? What was I wearing? How I did feel emotionally?
4. How did time pass? Fast or slow?
5. Was I thinking about anything in particular?
6. Where was my focus? Was it on the competitors or on myself? Was I looking at things in my environment, or was I more quiet and inside myself?
7. Finally, put it all together and relive the moment in your mind.

You can also imagine your "worst performance" and answer the same questions as above. Afterward, compare the two images and notice differences. Use this information as a learning, and make changes accordingly.

**Action steps:**
- State what you do want rather than what you don't want. The way to be sure is to complete this sentence: "I want to_____."
- Brain cell growth never stops! Feed your brain thoughts that match your desired outcome.
- Do 5- to 10-minute daily meditations on a best performance.
- Remember that mindfulness is about awareness. You ultimately decide where to put your focus.

---

*"The best way to cope with mistakes is to learn from them and see yourself making changes. The worst way to cope with mistakes is to continually imagine them."*
—Kristine Eiring, Ph.D.

---

# Chapter 5
## Meditations

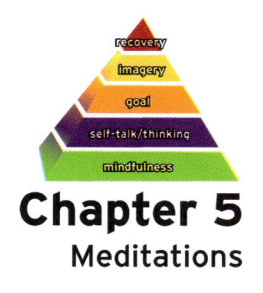

*"When we achieve the right focus, when we are properly mindful of what we're doing, awareness and action merge."*
—James Loehr, Ed.D.

Many athletes who have not been part of a meditation practice might have some preconceived ideas of what meditation is. In this chapter we will review meditation in general terms and then describe two specific types of meditation that you can try on your own.

First, why should you care about meditation if you are an athlete?

Because current research in showing us that meditation is associated with changes in brain structure (Holzel, et al., 2011). Researchers at Massachusetts General Hospital, found that one area of the brain affected by meditation is the prefrontal cortex, which is involved in executive functions such as planning, decision-making, judgment, comparison of ideas, and memories. This area of the brain also affects performance. Though this research is considered preliminary, we're gaining ground in our understanding of the value of meditation.

There are many forms of meditation. Some are based on a way of living, such as meditations grounded in Buddhism or Zen practices. Some meditations are not based on spiritual, religious, or philosophical practice. Instead, they have been developed as relaxation tools.

Some basics to know about a meditation practice include misunderstandings that include:

- There is one correct method
- I should NOT have any thoughts
- I can't sit still for very long therefore I am not a good at this
- I think even more and this is wrong (likely to occur as you are now building awareness).

Below are examples of different types of meditations and you may want to try several methods to determine if there is one you prefer for building mental focus.

**Simple Breathing Meditation**

Sit or lay down in a comfortable position. Take a few moments to get comfortable and begin to be aware of your breathing. As you breath in, say "I am breathing in" and as you breath out say, "I am breathing out". Focus your awareness on simply naming your breathing. Thoughts will creep in, make NO judgement about the thoughts, just return to naming your breathing. You can simplify the naming to "in" and "out". Begin this practice as a 5 minute meditation and work towards 10 or more minutes. This is a powerful brain training exercise making you aware of your thoughts and ability to focus. You will have thoughts, but the primary goal is to return your attention to naming the breath. This is the beginning of redirecting thoughts, which is a critical skill at performance time.

**Body Scan Meditation**

*Tip: record this meditation on your smartphone/mp3 player and listen to the recording as a guided meditation.

Lie down and breathe in slowly and deeply through your nose. Feel your abdomen move out and up as your diaphragm contracts and draws air into your lungs. Your chest should not rise noticeably. Repeat this deep breath 2 times.

Now as you breathe in, direct your attention to your left foot. Feel your foot. Wiggle your toes and become aware of how your left foot feels.

As you breathe in through your nostrils, slowly scan your left leg from foot to knee. Feel the sensations in your lower leg. Simply become aware of them. Accept any tension or discomfort. Scan slowly, up through your thigh now.

As you breathe out, bring your awareness from your leg back down to your foot. Do this 3 times, with awareness of the sensations you feel in your left leg. If thoughts appear, then simply name them as "thoughts." Gently come back to your breath, and shift awareness over to your right foot.

Slowly inhale while scanning through your right calf, knee, and thigh. Exhale and scan back down s-l-o-w-l-y. Do this 3 times, with awareness of the sensations you feel in your right leg. Simply accept all sensations, name them, and feel what happens. Relax.

Now focus on your stomach. Feel it rising as you breathe in and sinking as you exhale. Your heart rate will begin to slow down. This is normal. Remain aware of your breath and your stomach as it moves up and down. Become aware of any sensations. Relax.

Now follow the same procedure with your left hand and arm as you did with your leg. You may clench your fist at first to really direct your awareness to your left hand. Breathe in and scan your arm beginning at your hand and moving upward toward your shoulder. Exhale and scan your arm slowly back down toward your hand. Do this 3 times.

Now scan up along the length of your right arm, to your shoulder, and then back down your arm to your hand. Breathe and scan your right arm 3 times.

Bring your awareness back up to your chest. Continue scanning up along your neck and to your face. *Gently* clench your jaws, and release as you exhale. Feel the sensations in your jaw and your throat. Breathe and scan. Feel how the back of your head rests against the floor. Scan your head.

**Now detach from focusing on any body parts.** Breathe. Feel how everything is connected, resting gently on the floor. Just breathe, letting any sensation come to you. Accept it as a part of you, and name it. Return to your breathing. You are big, and these sensations are only small parts of you. They fluctuate, come and go.

Just breathe for a minute and feel your body. Then sit up slowly.

---

*"The breath is the intersection of the body and mind."*
–Thich Nhat Hanh
*Breath Meditation (St. Ruth, 1998)*

---

# Chapter 6
## The Mindfulness-Body Connection and Recovery

*"You must be 100% committed to each action.
If there are doubts in your mind,
your muscles won't know what to do."*

– Gary Mack from his book Mind Gym

**Mindfulness and Recovery**

Have you ever downloaded a CD to an MP3 player? This process allows you to take music from one source and transfer it to a more portable outlet. Think of recovering from an athletic event as "downloading" important information you want to store and transfer to your next event.

**Why is recovery important?**

Among athletes, recovery isn't talked about very much. Our event ends and we shower, eat, and move on with life without taking the time to mindfully recover. But here is what may happen subconsciously:

We finally are quiet, usually at bedtime, and thoughts about our performance and things that did not go well creep into our minds. That activates a tension pattern in our brain and muscles. Then, at the next event, faster than the speed of light, our subconscious mind remembers the "bad" things and tension again forms in our body. We may become anxious, wondering, "What if the things that went wrong last time happen again?" These thoughts and physical reactions to memories happen quickly—all before we know it! This is why recovering with mindfulness is vital to athletic success.

Here's how to create a mindful recovery plan after an event:

1. Restorative pose (see image): Following your event, allow your heart rate to return to a normal rhythm, and then make your way into restorative pose. Sit directly next to a wall and lay on your back while raising your feet up the wall. Place a pillow or blanket under your hips if that's more comfortable for you. Position your legs as close to the wall as possible, allowing your feet to rest against the wall. Note: If you suffer from back pain or strain, check with your trainer or doctor before trying this pose.

2. Begin deep breathing by inhaling through your nose to a slow count of 5. Then exhale strongly out your mouth to a slow count of 7. Repeat this breathing exercise 3 times, and proceed to step 3 while remaining in restorative pose.

3. Apply the three A's while in restorative pose: awareness, acceptance, and action.

    - Awareness and acceptance begin with deep breathing.
    - Ask yourself three questions during your recovery:
        1. What went well?
        2. What did not go well?
        3. What will I need to do better next time?

- Action: Spend approximately 10 minutes in restorative pose. When you rise, immediately write down your answers to the three questions. Do this after every training session and competition. The more you repeat this process, the greater success you will achieve.

Pick three things you did well during an event and fill in the chart below. Then write each one on a green sticky note, and post the notes in places where you will see them throughout the week, such as on the bathroom mirror or car dashboard, or in a locker or desk. This is how to review a performance and help improve your next one!

What went well?_____

What did not go well?_____

What will I do better next time? _____

There is a theory in psychology that when you begin to think negatively or have fearful thoughts, your body develops muscle tension. That's another example of the mind-body connection. You don't want to end your day with thoughts that create tension. You want to be mindful of knowing when to switch your thinking—and how.

If you drive a car with the parking brake on, the efficiency of the car is decreased. The engine works well, but the output is slowed down. The same is true for how our thoughts affect our body. Fearful thoughts slow us down and can create tension in the body. Many fearful thoughts begin with "what if" statements:

What if Coach didn't like my performance?

What if this happens again in the future?

What if I keep missing my shot?

What if my serve is bad next time?

"What if" thoughts are associated with anxiety, muscle tension, and a decreased ability to think quickly in a situation. To work through "what if" thoughts, end your practice or training with mindfulness, and use recovery to help you improve your athletic performance. Review the chart below for ways to replace anxious or "mind-less" thoughts with mindful thoughts.

## Remember: A relaxed mind = a relaxed body.

| Mindful-less Thoughts | Mindful Thoughts |
|---|---|
| I can't... | I am strong. |
| What if I fail? | I have a relaxed focus on.... |
| I always perform badly at this location. | I am breathing. |
| I am never going to... | I see my green reminder, which means go! |

Here is space for you to write your own thoughts based on your sport:

| Mindful-less Thoughts | Mindful Thoughts |
|---|---|
|  |  |
|  |  |

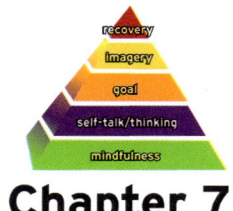

# Chapter 7
## Final Thoughts

*"When your heart is in the game, you have passion. When you have passion, your heart is in the game. Either way, you will most easily have mindfulness with heart and passion."*

–Kristine Eiring, Ph.D.

After reading this book, you have the tools you need to begin training your brain to be fully in the moment. Mindfulness is an ongoing process. You'll get better at it with practice and time, but be patient with yourself as you go.

One day soon, you'll find yourself applying the principles of mindfulness without having to remind yourself to do so. You'll experience flow, fully enjoying the present moment. And when you do, you'll most likely find yourself performing more successfully, too. The best performances occur when you are present–not regretting the past or worrying about the future or the outcome of the event.

Mindfulness is the greatest tool you have as an athlete, and it can take you to new places in training and competition. But mindfulness can also reignite your passion, your sense of fun.

Think back to when you first experienced the sports you compete in today. Where you a child? A teenager? And did you go into the sport dreaming of great success, or did you pick up the sport because you thought it was fun?

Chances are, you were drawn to a sport because you enjoyed it. But as we advance in a sport and become more serious competitors, we often lose that sense of fun—of pure passion.

Through mindfulness, you can find your way back. When you're not judging your performance, when you're focusing on the sheer movement of your body and the skills you've developing, you're experiencing the sport as you once did: the way you did as a child. You're remembering what you enjoyed about the sport, and letting go of what you don't.

So be in the present. Reignite your passion. Practice mindfulness, and see where it will take you!

# Appendix

Remember, **the first step to change is awareness**. Use these worksheets to help you develop awareness in your sport.

### Using Imaging/Visualization to Build Your Awareness

1. Do you visualize a successful performance?


2. Do you place yourself in the visualization?


3. Are you aware of how to create your own positive images to help you?


4. Do you picture what you don't want to happen? (If so, stop-and refocus on what you do want).


5. Do you imagine how you want to feel during your practice or competition?


6. Do you involve all your senses?

**Awareness of Your Best Performance**

1. Where was your focus right before you competed? Did you have a routine you followed?

2. Where was your focus during your competition?

3. What kept you connected to the present moment?

4. What did time feel like? Did it pass quickly or slowly?

5. Did you use any mental tools that helped you succeed?

6. Describe the sensation of "flow" or of being "in the zone."

**Mindfulness and Confidence Building**

1. Do you believe you can reach your goals?

2. Are you talking to yourself in ways that make you feel confident?

3. Do you know what to say to yourself to help your confidence grow?

4. Are you able to receive compliments?

5. Do you use recovery tools to help you recall your gains, growths, and successes?

# References

Cormier, S. & Nurius, P. (2008). Interviewing and change strategies for helpers. Pacific Grove, CA: Brooks/Cole-Thomson.

Davis, M., Eshelman, E. R. & McKay, M. (2006). The relaxation and stress reduction workbook. Oakland, CA: New Harbinger Publications.

Eliot, J. (2005). Motivation: The need to achieve. In Shane Murphy (Ed.), The sport psych handbook. (pp. 3-18). Champaign, IL: Human Kinetics.

Gardner, F. L., & Moore, Z. E. (2007). The psychology of enhancing human performance: The mindfulness-acceptance-commitment (MAC) approach. New York: Springer Publishing Company.

Gregg, M. & Hall, C. (2006). The relationship of skill level and age to the use of imagery by golfers. Journal of Applied Sport Psychology, 18(4), 363-375.

Harwood, C. (2005). Goals: more than just the score. In Shane Murphy (Ed.), The sport psych handbook. (pp. 19-36). Champaign, Il: Human Kinetics.

Holzel, B.K., Carmody, C., Vangel, M., Congleton, C., Yerramsetti, S. M., Gard, T., & Lazar, S. (2011). Mindfulness practice leads to increases in regional brain gray matter density. Psychiatry Research: Neuroimaging, 191(1): 36 DOI: 10.1016/j.pscychresns.2010.08.006

Kabat-Zinn, J. (1990). Full catastrophe living. New York, NY: Dell Publishing.

Loehr, J. (1982). Mental toughness training for sports. Lexington, MA: The Stephen Greene Press.

Mack, G. (2001). Mind gym. An athlete's guide to excellence. New York, NY: McGraw-Hill.

Mezey, E., Chandross K. J., Harta, G.,Maki, R. A. & McKercher, S. R. (2000). Turning blood into brain: Cells bearing neuronal antigens generated in vivo from bone marrow. Science, 2001 Apr20: 292, 438-440.

Sternberg, E. (2000). The balance within: The science connecting health and emotions. W.H. Freeman and Company, New York, NY.

St. Ruth, D. (1998). Sitting: A guide to Buddhist meditation. New York, NY: Penguin Group.

Vealey, R. & Greenleaf, C. (2006). Seeing is believing: Understanding and using imagery in sport. In Jean M. Williams (Ed.), Applied sport psychology. (pp. 306-343). New York: NY: McGraw-Hill.

Printed in Great Britain
by Amazon